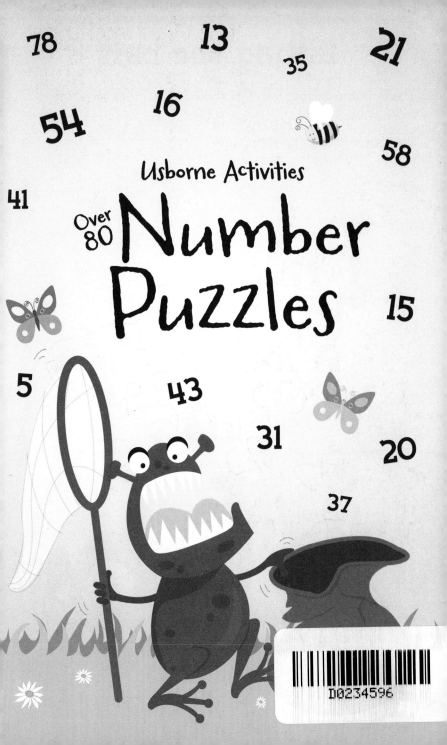

78

13

21

35

16

54

58

Usborne Activities

Over 80 **Number Puzzles**

41

15

5

43

31

20

37

D0234596

Taking the bait

These fish will only swallow the hook numbers that are 75% of the numbers on their bodies. Draw a circle around the fish that won't get hooked.

Bridge crossing

Only planks with calculations that are correct will hold your weight. Cross out the planks you should avoid to cross the bridge safely.

$40 \div 8 = 4$ ✗

$15 \times 3 = 45$ ✓

$58 - 33 = 24$ ✗

$45 + 23 = 68$ ✓

$52 \times 4 = 208$ ✗

$225 - 197 = 29$ ✗

$(51 - 6) \div 9 = 5$ ✓

$(68 \div 4) \times 3 = 51$ ✓

Pyramid puzzle

There are numbers missing from this pyramid. Write the missing numbers on the blank stones. Each number is the sum of the two directly underneath it.

Treasure chests

A chest contains treasure if the number on it is:

... a multiple of seven, or

... a square number, or

... a prime number.

Confuse the pirates by marking with an X the chests that don't have any treasure inside them.

Petal puzzle

Fill in the missing numbers so that both parts of each petal add up to the number in the middle.

Penguin population

Half of these penguins lay an egg, and each egg hatches a chick. When these chicks grow up, two thirds of them will lay an egg of their own, and each egg will hatch another chick. How many penguins will there be in total?

Answer: ....

Seat numbers

The Wilsons have bought tickets for a ballet. They'll all
be sitting together, and the numbers of the seats they've
booked add up to their joint age. Mrs. Wilson is 32 years
old and her husband is two years older. Their two children
are nine and seven. Draw crosses on the seats they'll sit in.

Crazy golf

Add up the scores on this crazy golf scorecard and find out who won the game (the player with the lowest score). Underline the winning player.

CRAZY 9
Scorecard

Hole name	Player 1	Player 2	Player 3
1. Toadstool	5	3	4
2. Molehill	4	5	4
3. Top Hat	6	5	7
4. Rickety Bridge	7	8	6
5. Cannon	9	10	8
6. Castle Keep	8	7	8
7. Rose Cottage	8	9	9
8. Lighthouse	7	8	10
9. Windmill	10	8	9
TOTAL	99	63	65

18
19
20
21
19
20
21
22
82

Draw on the dice

Draw the correct number of spots on the blank dice to complete the calculations.

a.

([5] + [4]) ÷ [3] = 3

b.

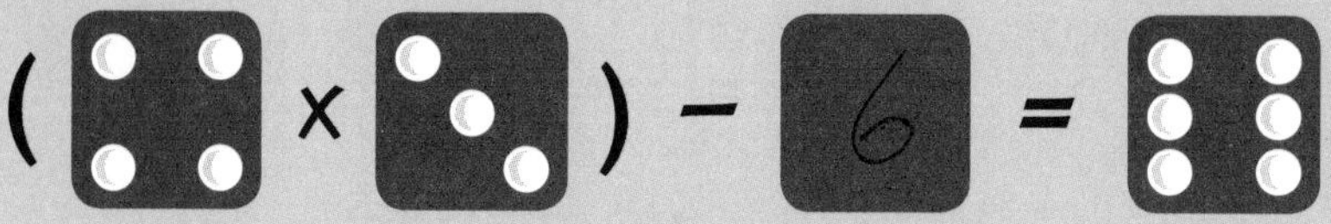

([4] × [3]) − 6 = [6]

c.

([4] ÷ [ ]) + [1] = [3]

d.

([ ] − [3]) × [3] = [4]

Strength test

Harry, Sam and Lisa tested their strength on the machine below. Harry and Sam went first and their scores flashed up on the machine. If Lisa's score was halfway between Harry's and Sam's, what did she score?

Answer:

125

? 113 177

Chocolate box

Decorate two thirds of these chocolates. How many are left blank?

Answer: ....5.............

Running total

Find each runner's total to see how quickly they will get around the track. The one with the highest total will cross the finish line first. Circle the winner.

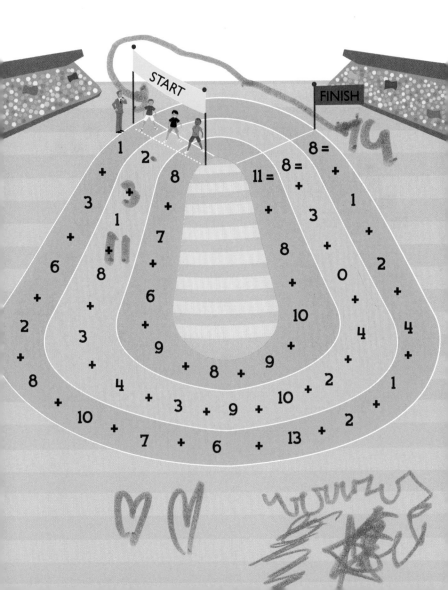

Robot scales

Take away three red boxes to balance the scales.
Cross out the ones you need to remove.

Butterfly wings

Fill in the missing numbers so that the number you make by multiplying the numbers on a butterfly's top wings is the same as you make by multiplying the numbers on its bottom wings. The first one has been done for you.

Alien panic

There's only time for three aliens to jump down each crater before the spaceship lands on Mars. How many are left out in the open?

Answer: 25

Archery training

Robin Hood's Merry Men have been testing their archery skills on these targets. Little John has ten arrows and hits his target with 80% of them. Will Scarlet has 16 arrows, of which 75% hit his target. 40% of Friar Tuck's 15 arrows miss his target. Whose target is whose? Write the correct letter under each person's name.

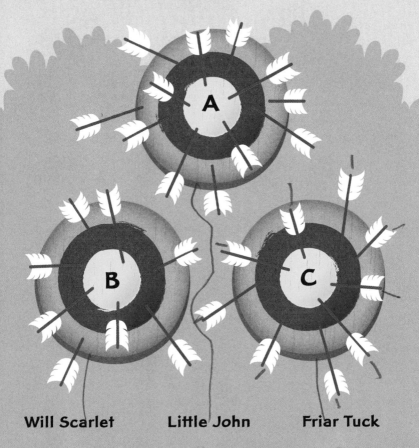

Will Scarlet

Little John

Friar Tuck

....

Squirrel's nest

Nutty the squirrel needs ten leaves to build her nest, but she can only use leaves with numbers that are multiples of nine. Circle the leaves she can use. Will she have enough to make her nest? Underline the correct answer at the bottom of the page.

Answer: Yes / No

T-shirt designs

Add patterns to these people's T-shirts so that: $\frac{1}{3}$ are plain black, 25% are dotted, $\frac{1}{4}$ are striped, and $\frac{1}{6}$ are left white. If you choose a person at random, what is the chance that their T-shirt will not be plain black? Circle the correct answer.

A 1 in 3 **B** 2 in 3 **C** 8 in 10 **D** 4 in 12

Secret mission

A microchip containing top secret data is hidden in the city park. Use the map on the opposite page and the instructions below to guide Agent Q to the right spot.

On the map, fill in:

- all the squares with coordinates that add up to an odd number.

- all the squares that give an answer of 16 or more when you multiply their coordinates.

- all the squares that give an answer of nine or less when you multiply their coordinates.

The remaining squares form two diagonal lines. The square between these lines is where the microchip is buried. Write its coordinates below the map.

| 1 | 2 | 3 | 4 | 5 | 6 | 7 | 8 |

1
2
3
4
5
6
7
8
9
10

Answer:...............................

Multiplying machine

Pick the correct odd and even number from the choices below to send through the machine to give the answer 65. Write one number on each dotted line.

Triangle addition

Write the numbers 1 to 9 in the circles without repeating a number. Each side of the triangle should add up to 17. Three numbers have already been filled in for you.

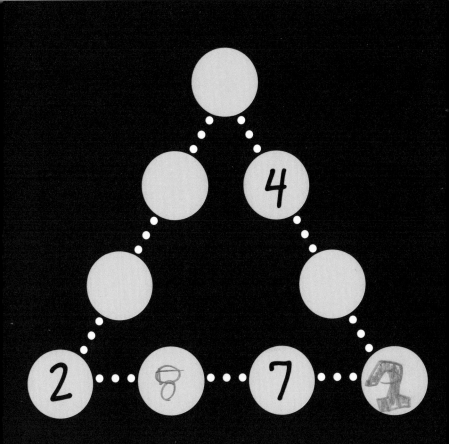

Duck maze

Help the duck get to her ducklings, subtracting from 200 the numbers she swims across along the way. What number are you left with?

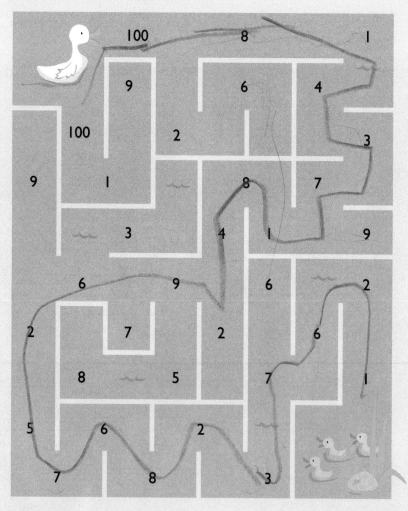

Answer:..............................

Cycle routes

Three friends leave their homes at the same time and cycle to the lake, taking different routes. Circle the cyclist who will reach the lake first if...

...**Charlie** cycles up and down one hill every ten minutes, but he has to go back home for his sandwiches, which adds 25 minutes to his time.

...**Benji** cycles up and down one hill every 11 minutes, but spends ten minutes fixing a puncture.

...**Sunil** cycles up and down one hill every 12 minutes, and he rides to the lake without stopping.

Missing symbols

Fill in the missing symbols to make each line true. Use < for "is less than", > for "is more than" or = for "is equal to".

a. 50.01 .... 50.1

b. $\frac{1}{3}$ .... $\frac{40}{120}$

c. 0.8 .... $\frac{3}{5}$

d. 40,400 .... four thousand and forty

e. −13 .... −14

f. 100,000 .... one million

g. 40% .... $\frac{1}{4}$

h. 3.5 .... $\frac{7}{2}$

i. $\frac{1}{6}$ .... $\frac{6}{30}$

j. Ninety-nine point nine 9.99

Racing cars

Can you work out what the missing racing car numbers should be?

Red: ....

Yellow: ....

Blue: ....

The number of spectators is a hundred times the sum of the car numbers that are prime. How many people are watching the race?

Answer: ....

Odd one out

Do the calculations, then underline
the odd one out in each set.

52 − 47

3.5 + 2.5

45 ÷ 9

1.25 x 4

2.75 x 4

9.25 + 1.75

79 − 68

72 ÷ 6

93 − 77

48 ÷ 3

5.25 x 3

6.5 + 9.5

16.5 + 4.5

4 x 5.5

110 ÷ 5

58 − 36

Hidden multiples

Fill in all the squares that contain a multiple of eight to reveal a hidden number in the grid. What can you see?

3	20	15	4	6	1	2	22
91	43	37	8	16	52	63	71
23	17	24	90	100	32	21	7
13	40	50	2	61	81	48	5
15	15	80	12	0	64	11	17
51	23	101	56	72	2	4	5
78	185	88	111	99	144	6	7
13	96	12	3	9	10	136	11
14	15	104	17	18	128	19	20
21	22	42	112	120	102	99	4
7	23	105	0	5	7	3	1

Monkey mayhem

Some monkeys have escaped from the zoo. See if you can find them all in the picture below, then answer these questions:

If a monkey is recaptured every 45 minutes, how many are still on the loose after three hours?

Answer: ....

After 12 hours, the zoo calls off the search. How many monkeys escape recapture?

Answer: ....

Apple packing

There are 20 times more apples than you can see here – and the farmer needs to pick and pack them all. He has ten large boxes, which each hold 20 apples, and 13 small boxes, which each hold 15 apples. He fills all the boxes, but has some apples left over. How many are left unpacked?

Answer:................................

Breaking the code

Agent 006 $\frac{1}{2}$ is trying to decode a top secret message sent by his mother. Can you use the information on the opposite page to help him find out what it says?

MESSAGE:

20	54	18	42

12	3	54	18

27	54	72	35	6

8.8	3	47	42

CODE

A=60% of 15   G=25% of 64

C=50% of 12   I=70% of 50

D=80% of 11   M=90% of 30

E=20% of 20   N=60% of 70

O=5% of 60   T=25% of 80

P=20% of 40   U=75% of 72

R=40% of 45   W=50% of 94

S=80% of 90   Y=6% of 200

Sequence search

Draw lines through the numbers that follow the sequences described below. The lines zigzag across either from left to right or right to left, as shown in the example. Each sequence is five numbers long.

1. **Count in 3s from 7.**
2. **Count in 2s from 60.**
3. **Count in 4s from 56.**
4. **Count in 6s from 41.**
5. **Count in 7s from 40.**

6		8		78		40		19
	10		16		2		7	
7		13		19		12		6
	72		64		56		64	
69		68		60		60		69
	6		17		41		9	
41		53		65		62		0
	47		59		40		72	
38		96		19		47		1
	72		41		66		62	
87		60		68		64		60
	56		47		61		12	
53		40		54		68		3
	20		53		99		11	

Street scene

In the picture below, the number of houses = H, the number of windows = W, the number of roofs = R, the number of chimneys = C, the number of plants = P and the number of doors = D.

Only three of these calculations are true.
Mark the false ones with an X.

1. $W \div R = P^2$ ....

2. $C + D = W - H$ ....

3. $H + R + P = W - C$ ....

4. $P \times C = D + R$ ....

5. $R + D = W \div P$ ....

Which bus?

Use this timetable to answer the questions below.

Departures						
Furnace Vale	08:35	09:00	09:15	09:35	09:55	10:20
Hayfield		09:20		09:55		10:40
New Mills	09:30	09:55	10:10	10:30	10:50	11:15
Brinnington	09:45	10:10		10:45	11:05	

Mike catches the 08:35 bus from Furnace Vale and stops off in New Mills for an hour and fifteen minutes. What time is the next bus to Brinnington that he can catch?

Answer: ....

Maddie wants to spend at least an hour in Hayfield, and then be in New Mills by 11:20. What time is the latest bus she can catch from Furnace Vale?

Answer: ....

Find fifteen

Write the numbers 1 to 9 in this grid without repeating a number. The numbers in each row and column should add up to 15. The first two numbers have already been filled in for you.

Butterfly farm

At the beginning of the month, there were
180 caterpillars at Green Valley Butterfly Farm.
70 were striped, 60 were spotted and 50
were hairy. By the end of the month, 21 of
the striped caterpillars, 15 spotted ones
and 16 hairy ones had transformed into
butterflies. What percentage of each
type of caterpillar had transformed?

Striped ....

Spotted ....

Hairy ....

Snip snip

Alice, Jess, Elsa and Beth visit the hairdresser. The hairdresser cuts off half of Alice's hair length. Jess has half as much hair cut off as Alice. Elsa has 25% less hair cut off than Alice. Beth has half as much hair cut off as Jess. Using the lines to help you, shade in the cut off amounts to restyle the girls' hair.

Who has the least hair cut off? Circle her name.

Alice   **Jess**   **Elsa**   **Beth**

Fruit puzzle

The chart at the bottom of the page tells you how many pieces of each fruit make one serving. If you eat three servings a day, how many days will the fruit supply below last?

Each of these pictures shows one serving of fruit:

Answer: ....

Snowflakes

If 11,000 snowflakes fall into a field every ten minutes, how many snowflakes will there be after two hours?

Underline the correct answer below:

a. Thirteen thousand, two hundred snowflakes

b. One hundred and thirty thousand, and two snowflakes

c. One thousand, three hundred and two snowflakes

d. One hundred and thirty-two thousand snowflakes

Pipes puzzle

Follow the calculation along the pipes, and write the answer to each stage in the red circles. What number will come out of the pipe? Write the final answer in the red box at the bottom of the page.

45

÷5 9 −6 ×4 12

×3

−13 +11 ÷4 36

×2

14 +7 −5 16 ÷8

+2

Alien growth spurt

These aliens measure their height in zoiks. If each alien grows ten zoiks a month until it is 60 zoiks tall, and five zoiks a month after that, who will be 75 zoiks tall in six months' time? Measure the aliens from the tops of their heads and then underline the correct one.

- 100zk
- 90zk
- 80zk
- 70zk
- 60zk
- 50zk
- 40zk
- 30zk
- 20zk
- 10zk

Naughty Kittens

Three kittens have run riot with paint on their paws.
Count the paw prints on the next page, then answer
the questions below.

If each paw print takes three minutes to scrub out,
how many minutes would it take to clean the
whole room?

Answer: ....

If the kittens leave this many paw prints in
six minutes, how many would they make in 15?

Answer: ....

If Smudge leaves twice as many paw prints as Pixie,
and Pixie leaves three times as many as Nelson,
how many paw prints does each cat make?

Smudge:............ **Pixie:**............ **Nelson:**............

Smudge

Pixie

Nelson

Jelly beans

Rico, Dan and Tom divide a pile of jelly beans between themselves according to their ages. Tom is the youngest and Rico is the oldest, and for every one bean that Tom gets, Dan gets two and Rico gets three. Count the jelly beans to find out how many each boy gets.

Rico:............... **Dan:**............... **Tom:**...............

Prime gobbler

The prime gobbler eats up anything that's a prime number. Circle the numbers that he **won't** eat.

Hidden silhouette

Fill in the shapes that contain the numbers divisible by four. What can you see?

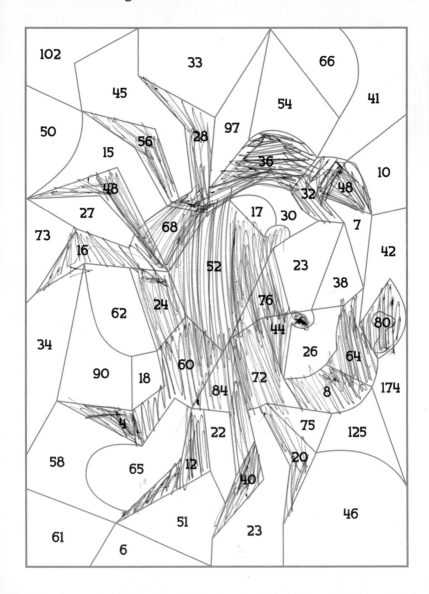

Bird spotting

In a survey of rainforest birds, a researcher sees:

• **5 red birds**   • **6 blue birds**   • **1 gold bird**

His assistant sees:

• **3 red birds**   • **8 blue birds**   • **5 pink birds**   • **4 green birds**

What percentage of the researcher's birds are blue?

Answer: ....

What percentage of the assistant's birds are pink?

Answer: ....

What percentage of all the birds they both see are red?

Answer: ....

Snakes and ladders

Tim and Anna are playing snakes and ladders. Solve the calculations to find out where they land. Draw circles for Tim's counter and triangles for Anna's, erasing the old counters as you move along. Underline the winner's name.

Tim

Turn one: $24 \div 12$

Turn two: $\frac{3}{2} + \frac{5}{2}$

Turn three: $10.5 - 8.5$

Turn four: $\frac{8}{4} + 3$

Anna

Turn one: $2 - \frac{15}{15}$

Turn two: $18 \div 3$

Turn three: $\frac{3}{2} + \frac{3}{2}$

Turn four: $1.5 + 2.5$

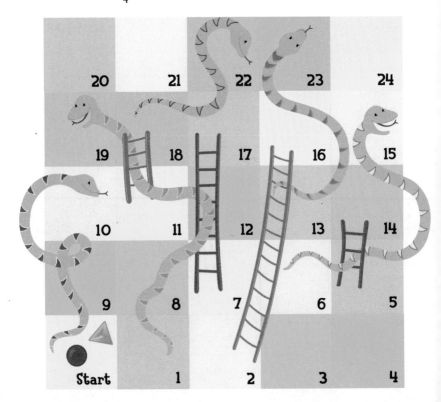

Short leash

The puppy in the picture below is attached to a leash. He can only move 23 steps from his owners before the leash runs out. Draw a circle around the toys he can reach.

13 steps

11 steps

15 steps

11 steps

14 steps

12 steps

9 steps

10 steps

15 steps

12 steps

14 steps

13 steps

Counting coins

A boy goes to a funfair with a jingling pocketful of coins. He spends a third of them on ice cream, then he goes on a rollercoaster and loses half of the coins he had left. Now he has only nine coins. How many did he have to start with?

Answer:..

Caterpillar counting

Fill in the missing numbers to complete each sequence.

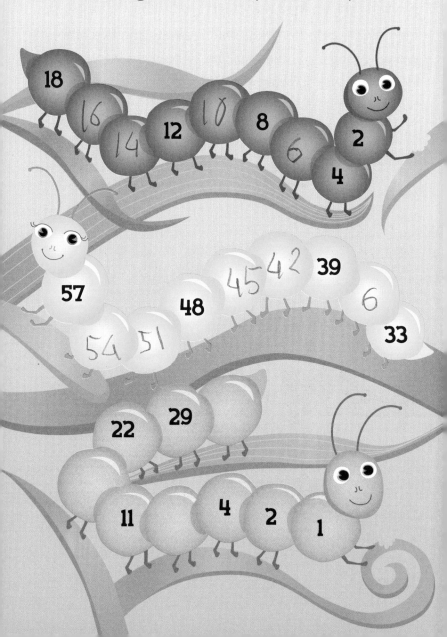

Perching birds

This flock of birds has settled on some telephone wires. At 8:00pm, some of the birds will fly away, but six will join the flock. At 8:15, ten birds will fly away, and five others will arrive. By 8:30, there will be 26 birds on the wires. How many will fly away at 8:00pm?

Answer:...........................

Cops and robbers

Which is the getaway car? Help the police car find it by taking the road with the question that gives the lowest answer at each turn. Underline the correct car.

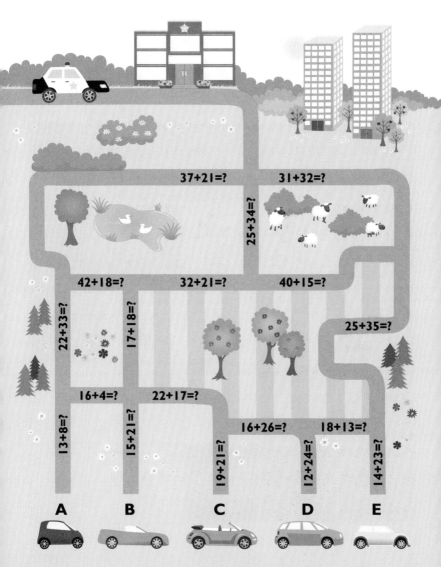

37+21=?

31+32=?

25+34=?

42+18=?

32+21=?

40+15=?

22+33=?

17+18=?

25+35=?

16+4=?

22+17=?

13+8=?

15+21=?

16+26=?

18+13=?

19+21=?

12+24=?

14+23=?

A   B   C   D   E

Cross sum

Fill in the blank squares with numbers from 1 to 9. The numbers in each row or column should add up to the total shown on the arrows. (The direction of the arrows shows you whether to add across or down the grid.) You can only use a number once in an answer. For example, you can make 4 with 3 and 1, but not with 2 and 2.

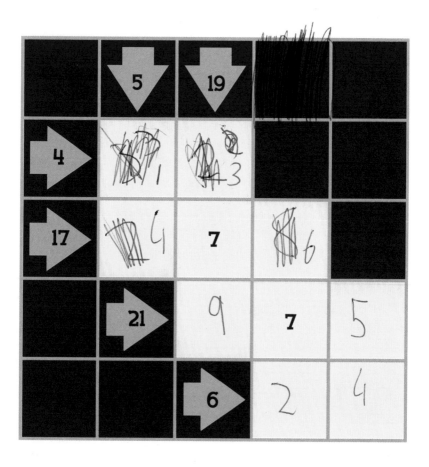

Coconut collecting

Every time Beaky the parrot lands on a branch of one of these trees, six coconuts fall down. The pirate gives her one third of the coconuts she's collected, and eats the rest. If Beaky lands on each of the branches once, how many coconuts will the pirate have for dinner?

Answer: ....

Mayan code

An ancient South American people called the Mayans used number symbols made from dots and dashes. Some of them are shown below. Can you fill in the missing symbols?

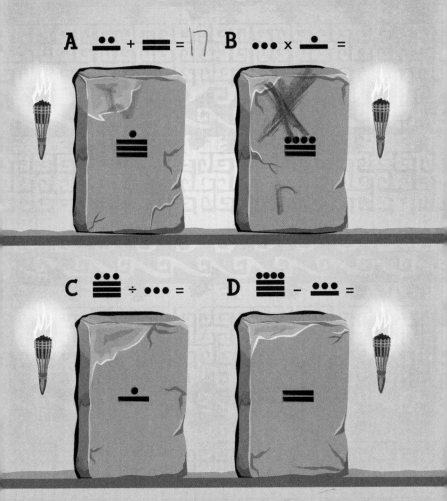

Complete the code on the previous page, then use it
to find out which door hides the treasure of an ancient
Mayan king. The treasure is behind the door carved with
the correct answer to the calculation on the wall above it.
Mark the door with an X.

Cross-number

12 000 +240

Use the clues to put the correct numbers into the grid.

	¹2	4	²0	0	
			8		
³			⁴4	0	⁵5
			5		
⁶2	0	3	0		
			3		

Across →

1. The number of minutes in two days

4. Five thousand, six hundred minus five thousand, one hundred and ninety-five

6. The number of toes in a room of 406 people

Down ↓

2. Eight hundred and four thousand, five hundred and three

3. One thousand and twenty-one plus four hundred and nineteen

5. The number of legs on 141 sheep

Number search

The answers to the questions at the bottom
of the page are hidden in the grid. They may
be written in any direction. When you find
each one, draw around it, as shown here.

7	3	9	2	0
4	8	0	8	1
0	2	5	3	7
4	6	3	8	7
8	1	5	0	9

0	4	1	6	5	0	7	2
2	7	0	9	9	9	1	5
1	9	2	6	3	0	9	4
4	5	0	9	5	1	6	8
4	6	1	2	5	0	7	1
7	0	7	1	9	8	8	2
9	3	4	0	3	1	6	3
7	7	6	0	4	9	8	1

(36 ÷ 9) x 12 = ?   (9 x 6) + 23 = ?   (71 + 21) ÷ 4 = ?

(24 x 5) – 7 = ?   (32 – 8) x 6 = ?   (84 ÷ 7) x 9 = ?

(99 – 29) ÷ 2 = ?   (10 + 5) x 11 = ?   (53 + 67) ÷ 5 = ?

Counting sheep

On Sunday, Ben counted 64 sheep to help him fall asleep. He counted half as many on Monday, and then each night for the rest of the week he counted five fewer than the night before. How many sheep did Ben count before he fell asleep on Saturday?

Answer:..

Blast off

Complete the code to launch the rocket.

1 : 3 : 6 : 10 : 15 : .... : ....

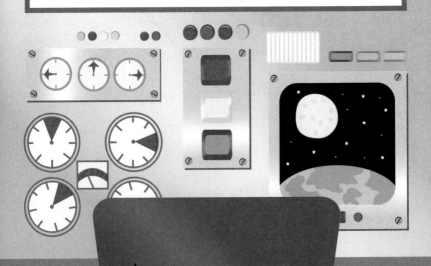

Bingo

Aman and Sarah are playing bingo. They cross out a calculation on their card when its answer is called out. Play the game and draw a star next to the winning card.

"86, 35, 48, 7, 36, 25, 22, 46, 90, 43, 85"

BINGO CARD - Aman

4x12	62–19	66÷3	9x10
6x6	225÷9	52+33	99–13

BINGO CARD - Sarah

38–3	101–15	7x4	21+25
6x8	110÷5	52+38	49÷7

Gymnasts

These gymnasts have all been awarded a score for their performances. Use the equation at the bottom of the page to find out how many points Amy was given. Write her score under her name.

Maggie

3
....

Flora

7
....

Cara

5
....

Amy

6.3
....

Cattle round-up

Billy Bronca is rounding up his cattle, but he can only lasso the animals whose numbers match one of the numbers on his hat. Draw around the cattle he catches.

Tables test

Four friends each had a times tables test at school.
Who scored the highest? Check the girls' answers, give
them each a score and draw a star on the winning sheet.

Name ..... Maisie .....

1x9= 9 ✓   6x9= 54 ✓
2x9= 18 ✓   7x9= 61
3x9= 27 ✓   8x9= 72
4x9= 37 ✗   9x9= 83 ✗
5x9= 45   10x9= 90 ✓

Score ⁷/10

Name ..... Laura .....

1x7= 7 ✓   6x7= 42 ✓
2x7= 14 ✓   7x7= 39 ✗
3x7= 20 ✗   8x7= 55 ✗
4x7= 28 ✓   9x7= 63 ✓
5x7= 33 ✗   10x7= 70 ✓

Score ⁶/10

Name ..... Becky .....

1x4= 4 ✓   6x4= 24 ✓
2x4= 8 ✓   7x4= 28 ✓
3x4= 12 ✓   8x4= 34 ✗
4x4= 16 ✓   9x4= 36 ✓
5x4= 20 ✓   10x4= 40 ✓

Score ⁹/10

Name ..... Kate .....

1x6= 6 ✓   6x6= 36 ✓
2x6= 12 ✓   7x6= 42
3x6= 18   8x6= 48
4x6= 24 ✓   9x6= 54
5x6= 30 ✗   10x6= 60

Score ⁸/10

Leaving home

Max the mouse has spent $\frac{1}{2}$ of his life being chased by a cat, $\frac{1}{4}$ of his life being chased by a dog, and $\frac{1}{8}$ of his life avoiding mousetraps. But three weeks ago, he moved to a peaceful new house. How long did he spend doing each thing?

.... weeks running from the cat.

.... weeks running from the dog.

.... weeks avoiding mousetraps.

Max is .... weeks old.

A walk in the woods

Help Little Red Riding Hood reach Granny's cottage along the shortest route. She can only walk across clearings where the answer is an even number.

3 x 9 = ?

9 + 11 = ?

9 + 8 + 1 = ?

12 x 8 = ?

3 x 7 = ?

64 + 8 = ?

9 x 9 = ?

2 + 4 + 3 = ?

7 x 8 = ?

6 x 4 = ?

11 x 3 = ?

8 + 3 + 1 = ?

32 + 9 = ?

7 x 7 = ?

2 + 7 + 9 = ?

Honey bees

Each bee can only find nectar in flowers with a number that can be divided by its own. Draw a circle around the bee that doesn't have a flower.

Square addition

Write the numbers below in the red circles so that each side of the square adds up to 20 and all the numbers are used.

5 3 9 10

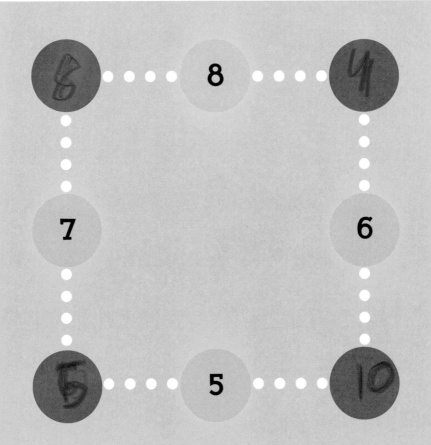

Stepping stones

Help Amina find her way across the stepping stones to the other side of the stream. She can only step on stones that have square numbers.

Number mix

Each purple potion number has been made by multiplying
a red potion number by a yellow one. If each number has
been used only once, circle the red and yellow potions that
haven't been used.

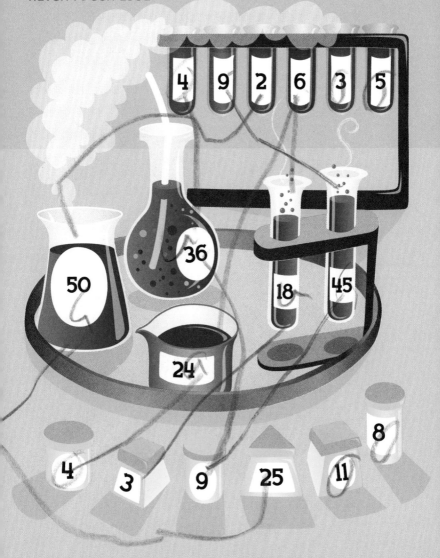

Santa's little helper

Daffy, the naughty elf, stole Santa's sleigh on Christmas Eve and tried to deliver the gifts by himself. By the time Santa caught him, he had dropped 70 gifts.

In the first five minutes of the flight, he dropped 20 gifts, but his aim was bad so only two in five went down the right chimney. How many reached their target?

Answer:..............................

He dropped the next 50 gifts while a strong wind was blowing, so there was 50% less chance of the gifts going down the right chimney. How many of them reached their target?

Answer:..............................

Dartboard scores

In this game of darts, you have to throw three darts into the dartboard and can only hit each section once. The inner sections on this dartboard are double the value of the outer ones.

a. What's the lowest score you can make? ...1...

b. What's the highest score you can make? ...26...

c. How many different ways can you reach a target score of ten with three darts? ....

Puppy maze

Help the puppy get to the bone, adding up the numbers it runs over along the way. Write the total at the bottom of the page.

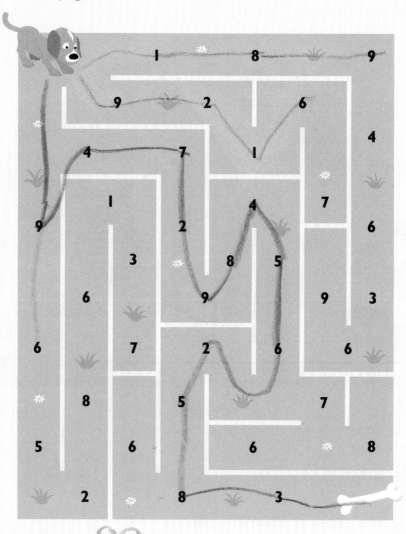

Answer: 82

Swirling in space

Add up all the numbers in this swirly calculation and write the grand total on the yellow moon.

1 + 2 + 3 + 4 + 5 + 6 + 7 + 8 + 9 + 10 + 11 + 12 + 13 + 14 + 15 + 16 + 17 + 18 + 19 + 20 + 21 + 22 + 23 + 24 + 25 + 26 + 27 + 28 + 29 + 30 + 31 + 32 + 33 + 34 + 35 + 36 + 37 + 38 + 39 + 40 + 41 + 42 + 43 + 44 + 45 + 46 + 47 + 48 + 49 + 50 =

Dominoes

How many of these dominoes have spots that add up to...

...an even number? ....

...a prime number? ....

...a multiple of three? ....

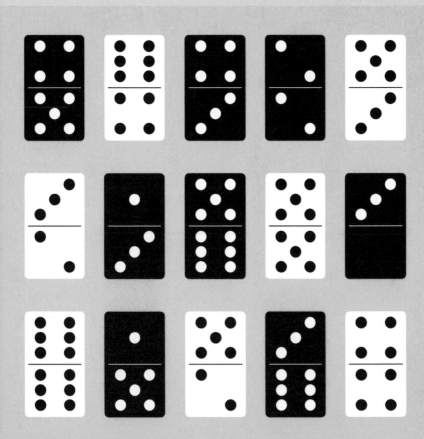

Sudoku

The grid is made up of nine blocks, each containing nine squares. Fill in the blank squares so that each block, row and column contains all the digits 1 to 9.

		9	8	6			5	3
6					9	8		
8	1			3			2	
	3	4			2	5		7
7			6		4	9		
5		8	7				1	
	9			2			7	6
		6	5	4				2
4	7				6	3		

Who's who?

Use the ages below and the following clues to see who's who. Lana is four months older than Meg, who is six months younger than Dan. Ali is two months younger than Meg and six months younger than Lana. Fill in the correct name under each person.

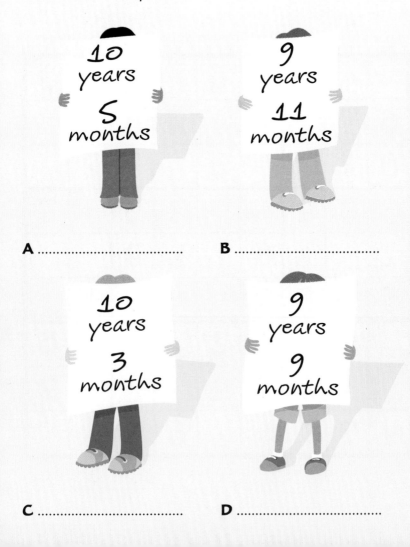

10
years
5
months

9
years
11
months

A ....

B ....

10
years
3
months

9
years
9
months

C ....

D ....

Rope ladder climb

Add up the numbers on each tree trunk and move that number of rungs up the tree's rope ladder. Circle the bunch of coconuts you will reach.

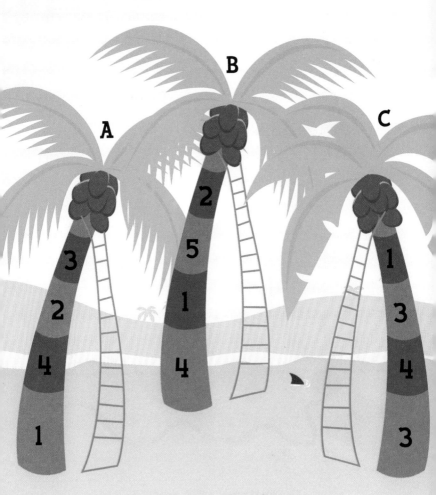

Toy sale

Bobby is selling his old toys to his friends. All the prices are in marbles. After a while, he reduces everything to half the marked price. Sometimes he has to round the new price up to the nearest whole marble. Write each new price in the correct space on the opposite page.

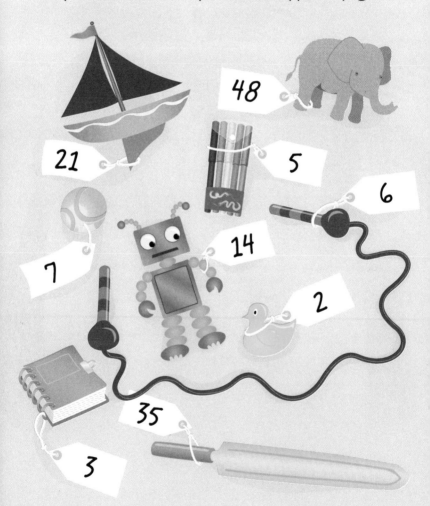

= ....   = ...

= ....    = ...

= ....    = ...

= ....   = ...

 = ...

Under the sea

These pictures of sea creatures stand for numbers. The fish is 13, the octopus is two, and the shark is six. What number does the crab represent?

Answer: ....

Compass points

Follow the descriptions to discover which three directions the compass needle points to during a journey. The needle starts at North (N).

Answers:

The needle swings 90° clockwise.	....
Then, it swings 180° in the opposite direction.	....
Lastly, it swings 45° clockwise.	....

Number muncher

The number muncher eats anything that's a multiple of six or seven. Circle the numbers he eats.

11 21 16 13 78

62 5 41

36 58 43

20

2 31

54 35

37 15 64

56 33

22

4 fill-in

Write the numbers 1, 2, 3 or 4 in the squares without repeating a number in any row or column. The number in each outlined set of squares should add up to the small number in the corner of the set. Some numbers have already been filled in for you.

7	2		4
			3
		3	
	5		3

Who am I?

Use the clue to uncover each mystery number, and write your answers on the dotted lines.

a. "If two is the first even number, I am the ninth, multiplied by three.

Who am I?"

b. "I am a prime number less than 20. My two digits added together make four.

Who am I?"

c. "I am the second square number multiplied by the third square number (if the first square number is one).

Who am I?"

Vending machine

A toy vending machine contains 30 toys. There are 15 aliens, one dinosaur and the rest are robots. Draw lines to join the questions below to their correct answers.

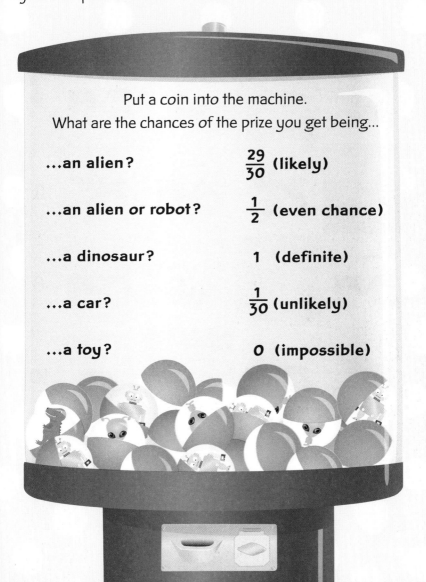

Put a coin into the machine.
What are the chances of the prize you get being...

...an alien? $\frac{29}{30}$ (likely)

...an alien or robot? $\frac{1}{2}$ (even chance)

...a dinosaur?   1 (definite)

...a car? $\frac{1}{30}$ (unlikely)

...a toy?   0 (impossible)

Picture code

Each picture below stands for a different number from 1 to 4. The numbers at the edges of the grid are the sum of the numbers in each row or column. Can you find out which picture represents which number?

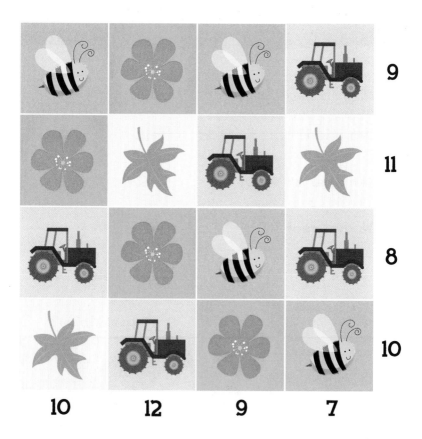

9

11

8

10

10 12 9 7

Answers:

 = ... = ...   = ... = ...

Catch the train

All of these trains take 19 minutes to reach your destination, but you need to arrive between 10:45 and 11:15. Write down the arrival time for each train, then draw an X on the train you need to catch.

Depart	10:58
Arrive	....

Depart	10:25
Arrive	....

Depart	11:00
Arrive	....

Depart	10:27
Arrive	....

Hidden picture

Fill in the shapes that contain the numbers divisible by three. What can you see?

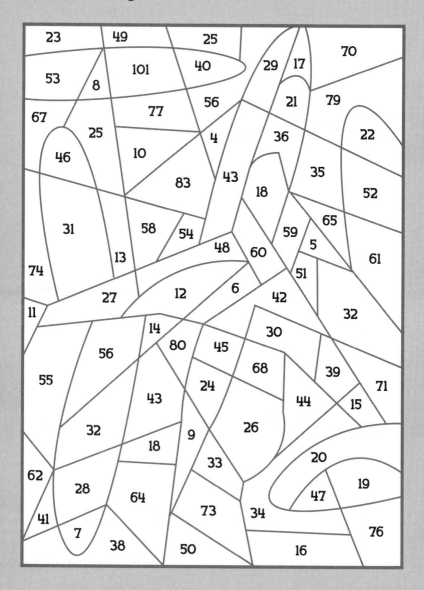

Number factory

How will the machine change the number on each box?
Write the new numbers on the boxes at the bottom.

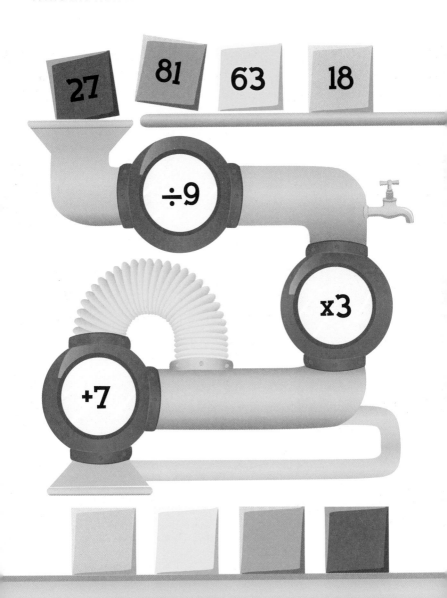

Missing symbols

Fill in the missing symbols to make each line true.
Use < for "is less than", > for "is more than" or = for "is equal to".

a. 200,020 .... two hundred thousand and two

b. $\frac{2}{3}$ 0.75

c. 2.25 .... $\frac{9}{4}$

d. eleven point one 11.01

e. –100 .... –99

f. $\frac{20}{80}$ .... $\frac{30}{90}$

g. 80.301 .... 80.098

h. 20% .... $\frac{3}{15}$

i. $\frac{7}{63}$ .... $\frac{1}{9}$

j. Five million 50,000,000

Sudoku

The grid is made up of nine blocks, each containing nine squares. Fill in the blank squares so that each block, row and column contains all the digits 1 to 9.

8		6	4		9	3	7	5
	2			8		1		6
3				6	2			
7	9		2		1		3	4
			8		4	7		
1	8		7		5		2	9
		8	3			5		7
6		1			7		8	
5	7	2						3

Find eighteen

Write the numbers 2 to 10 in this grid without repeating a number. The numbers in each row and column should add up to 18. The first two numbers have already been filled in for you.

Number search

The answers to the questions at the bottom of the page are hidden in the grid. They may be written in any direction. When you find each one, draw around it, as shown here.

4	0	9	5	7	8	6	7
1	2	4	8	0	3	9	4
3	8	7	1	6	5	4	0
7	4	0	2	8	0	6	6
0	7	2	3	9	4	3	3
1	1	8	3	5	2	0	7
3	2	0	5	9	4	8	2
4	5	8	9	2	7	9	1

$(106 - 28) \div 3 = ?$ $(59 - 27) \times 4 = ?$ $(9 \times 7) - 6 = ?$

$(102 \div 17) + 13 = ?$ $(9 + 14) \times 11 = ?$ $(12 \times 9) - 31 = ?$

$(21 - 15) \times 16 = ?$ $(39 + 45) \div 6 = ?$ $(112 - 22) \times 4 = ?$

Dividing machine

Pick the correct odd and even number from the choices below to send through the machine to give the answer eight. Write one number on each dotted line.

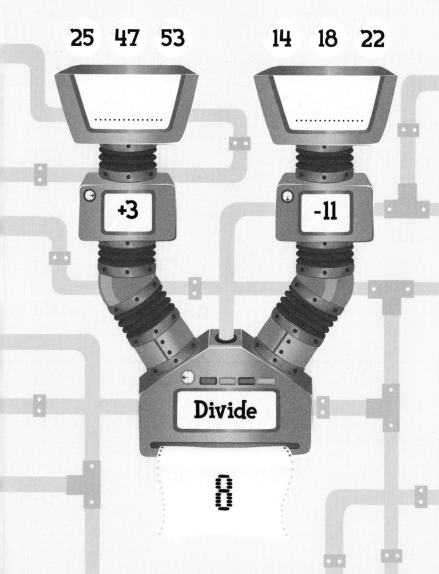

25 47 53   14 18 22

+3   -11

Divide

8

Snowflake puzzle

Fill in the missing numbers on the snowflakes so that both parts of each stem can be multiplied to give the number in the middle.

Cross sum

Fill in the blank squares with numbers from 1 to 9. The numbers in each row or column should add up to the total shown on the arrows. (The direction of the arrows shows you whether to add across or down the grid.) You can only use a number once in an answer. For example, you can make 4 with 3 and 1, but not with 2 and 2.

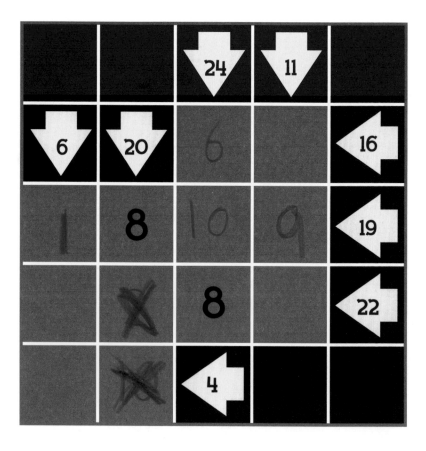

Beehive sequences

Draw lines through the numbers that follow the sequences described below. The lines zigzag across either from left to right or right to left, as shown in the example. Each sequence is five numbers long.

1. **Count down in 3s from 24.**
2. **Count down in 8s from 73.**
3. **Count down in 6s from 79.**
4. **Count down in 7s from 65.**
5. **Count down in 4s from 31.**

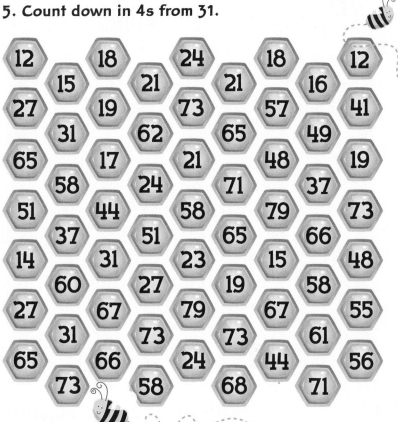

Hidden number

Solve each calculation on the left, then find the answer hidden in the number on the right. The first one has been done for you.

16 × 5　　=　　47⟨80⟩6

54 ÷ 2　　=　　32718

36 × 9　　=　　33324

78 − 23　　=　　55938

11 × 3　　=　　94533

91 + 30　　=　　112132

Domino chain

The dominoes at the bottom are missing from this chain. Decide where they should go, then add the spots in the right places.

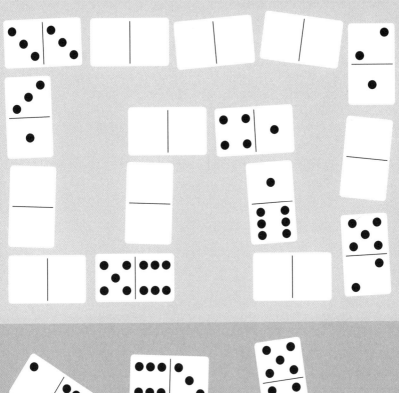

Scribbling space

You can use this page if you need more space to work out the answers to the puzzles.

Answers

1. Taking the bait:

2. Bridge crossing:
40 ÷ 8 = 4,   58 – 33 = 24,
225 – 197 = 29

3. Pyramid puzzle:

```
          222
       117   105
     68   49   56
   43   25   24   32
 27   16   9   15   17
15   12   4   5   10   7
```

4. Treasure chests:
8   15   44   69

5. Petal puzzle:

6. Penguin population: 33

7. Seat numbers:
19, 20, 21, 22

8. Crazy golf: Player 2

9. Draw on the dice:
a. b.  c. d.

10. Strength test: 145

11. Chocolate box: 5

12. Running total:

13. Robot scales:

| 35 | 7 | 1 |

14. Butterfly wings:

Answers

15. Alien panic: 5

16. Archery training:
Will Scarlet: A   Little John: B
Friar Tuck: C

17. Squirrel's nest: Yes

18. T-shirt designs: B

19. Secret mission:
4,4

20. Multiplying machine: 11 and 8

21. Triangle addition:
There are a few ways to do this puzzle. Here's one:

22. Duck maze: 0

23. Cycle routes: Benji

24. Missing symbols:
a. <   b. =   c. >   d. >   e. >   f. <
g. >   h. =   i. <   j. >

25. Racing cars:
Red: 11
Yellow: 15
Blue: 21
6,000 people

26. Odd one out:
3.5 + 2.5   72 ÷ 6
5.25 x 3   16.5 + 4.5

27. Hidden multiples:

Answers

28. Monkey mayhem:
16   4

29. Apple packing:
5

30. Breaking the code:
TURN YOUR MUSIC
DOWN

31. Sequence search:

32. Street scene:
2 and 4

33. Which bus?:
10:50
09:00

34. Find fifteen:

4	3	8
9	5	1
2	7	6

35. Butterfly farm:
Striped: 30%, Spotted: 25%
Hairy: 32%

36. Snip snip: Beth

Alice   Jess   Elsa   Beth

37. Fruit puzzle: 8 days

38. Snowflakes:
d. One hundred and thirty-two thousand snowflakes

39. Pipes puzzle:
9, 12, 36, 14, 16, 4

Answers

40. Alien growth spurt:

41. Naughty kittens:

180 minutes   150 prints

Smudge: 36   Pixie: 18

Nelson: 6

42. Jelly beans:

Rico: 15   Dan: 10   Tom: 5

43. Prime gobbler:

18, 27, 33, 65

44. Hidden silhouette:

45. Bird spotting:

50% blue 25% pink 25% red

46. Snakes and ladders:

Anna

47. Short leash:

48. Counting coins: 27

49. Caterpillar counting:

18, 16, 14, 12, 10, 8, 6, 4, 2

57, 54, 51, 48, 45, 42, 39, 36, 33

37, 29, 22, 16, 11, 7, 4, 2, 1

50. Perching birds: 5

51. Cops and robbers: D

52. Cross sum:

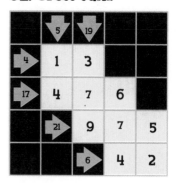

53. Coconut collecting: 36

Answers

54. Mayan code: C

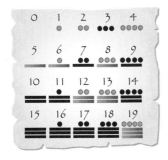

55. Cross-number:

		¹2	8	²8	0	
				0		
³1			⁴4	0	⁵5	
4			5		6	
⁶4	0	6	0		4	
0			3			

56. Number search:

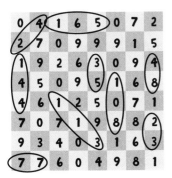

57. Counting sheep: 7

58. Blast off: 21 28

59. Bingo: Aman

60. Gymnasts: 2

61. Cattle round-up:
8^2, 11^2

62. Tables test:
Kate 10/10

63. Leaving home:
cat – 12 weeks
dog – 6 weeks
mousetraps – 3 weeks
Max is 24 weeks old.

64. A walk in the woods:

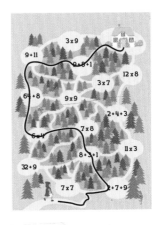

Answers

65. Honey bees: 14

66. Square addition:

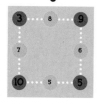

67. Stepping stones:

68. Number mix:

69. Santa's little helper:
8   10

70. Dartboard scores:

a.6   b.66   c.4

71. Puppy maze: 63

72. Swirling in space: 1,275

73. Dominoes: 8   5   5

74. Sudoku:

2	4	9	8	6	1	7	5	3
6	5	3	2	7	9	8	4	1
8	1	7	4	3	5	6	2	9
9	3	4	1	8	2	5	6	7
7	2	1	6	5	4	9	3	8
5	6	8	7	9	3	2	1	4
1	9	5	3	2	8	4	7	6
3	8	6	5	4	7	1	9	2
4	7	2	9	1	6	3	8	5

75. Who's who?: A. Dan
B. Meg   C. Lana   D. Ali

76. Rope ladder climb: C

77. Toy sale:

Answers

78. Under the sea: 23

79. Compass points:

E, W, NW

80. Number muncher:

21 35 36 54 56 78

81. 4 fill-in:

3	2	1	2
4	3	2	3
1	4	3	4
2	1	4	1

82. Who am I?:

a. 54   b. 13   c. 36

83. Vending machine:

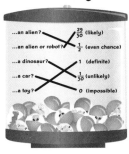

84. Picture code:

 =2   =4   =1   =3

85. Catch the train:

11:17   10:44   11:19   10:46

86. Hidden picture:

87. Number factory:

13   28   34   16

88. Missing symbols:

a. >   b. <   c. =   d. >   e. <

f. <   g. >   h. =   i. =   j. <

89. Sudoku:

8	1	6	4	2	9	3	7	5
4	2	7	5	8	3	1	9	6
3	5	9	1	7	6	2	4	8
7	9	5	2	6	1	8	3	4
2	6	3	8	9	4	7	5	1
1	8	4	7	3	5	6	2	9
9	4	8	3	1	2	5	6	7
6	3	1	9	5	7	4	8	2
5	7	2	6	4	8	9	1	3

Answers

90. Find eighteen:

There are a few ways to do this.
Here's one of them:

91. Number search:

92. Dividing machine: 53 and 18.

93. Snowflake puzzle:

94. Cross sum:

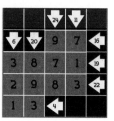

95. Beehive sequences:

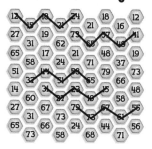

96. Hidden number:

27, 324, 55, 33, 121

97. Domino chain:

Written by Simon Tudhope and Sarah Khan
Designed by Marc Maynard and Michael Hill
Illustrated by Lizzie Barber and Non Figg

First published in 2014 by Usborne Publishing Ltd, 83–85 Saffron Hill, London ECIN 8RT, England.
Copyright © 2014 Usborne Publishing Ltd. The name Usborne and the devices ♀ ⊕ are Trade Marks of Usborne Publishing Ltd.
All rights reserved. No part of this publication may be reproduced, stored in a retrieval system, or transmitted in any form or by
any means, electronic, mechanical, photocopying, recording or otherwise, without the prior permission of the publisher. UE.